BACK FROM HELL

MERYDITH WILLOUGHBY

Willoughby, Merydith
BACK FROM HELL

ISBN 978-1-922803-55-9 (paperback)

LIVING LIFE & LOVING IT

While Merydith Willoughby has used her best efforts in preparing this book, she does not make any representation, whether implied or otherwise about the accuracy or completeness of the contents of this book or the application of the book's contents to the reader's personal situation. The information and strategies contained in this book may not be suitable for your situation and no advice is given as to what you should or should not do in relation to what is written in this book whatsoever. Any resemblance to actual persons or events is coincidental.

First edition 2010
Second edition 2022
Images from www.shutterstock.com

To purchase books and to schedule sessions contact:
Merydith Willoughby
Executive advisor
www.linkedin.com/in/merydithwilloughby
info@merydithwilloughby.com
New York City 718 790 9729
Australia 61 435086641

Typesetting Aileron Regular 10/18
Book edited and designed by Green Hill Publishing

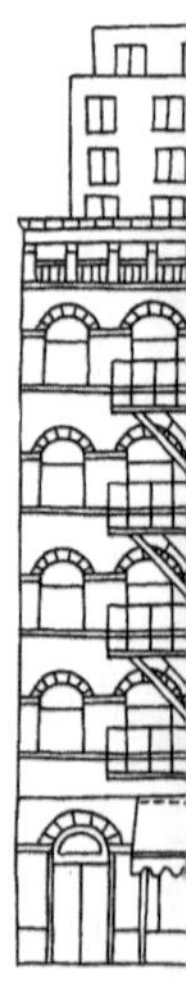

NYC COFFEE HOUSE

CONTENTS

BACK FROM HELL

It is a pleasure and a privilege to have written this second edition of *Back from Hell*. The reconstruction that had to occur for me to be able to do so, and the years that it has taken to regain my health and be better than I have ever been in some ways, has flawed me. There are many stages to burnout, and I had hit rock bottom - a point that, in reality, was very unlikely that I would ever return from. *Yes, things were that dire*. I have had to unpack who I am as a human being and who I am biologically.

1

I have learned much, worked tirelessly, and questioned every single thing that I was advised to do. Most of that was not of use, and I became my own practitioner and sourced professionals that could assist me to fully rebuild my human infrastructure. This process is discussed at length in my fourth book, *Thought Leadership*, as to what modality was used. I am now *living my life & loving it,* and I hope that you never, ever allow yourself to burnout as I did. If you are on the road to burnout, take note of what can occur and stop it before you descend into your own version of *Back from Hell*.

MERYDITH WILLOUGHBY

I t has taken me my whole life to work out this 'burnout' stuff, and some of the insights that I needed only came after I had written book four, *Thought Leadership*. Only then did I really get-me. I now know that it's not *if* I will burnout, but *when*. It is always just-around the corner; that is my biology – how I am hard-wired. I have now put strategies in place to ensure that it never, ever happens again, and they are monitored closely. I continue to challenge the status quo and to challenge current thinking, beliefs, and practices. I do not sit in front of anyone – professional or other – and allow them to dictate to me about what is possible, what I should do, or how I should live my life. I am in control of my destiny and take this very seriously.

3

We live in a period dominated by a mainstream that disrespect the capacity or even the possibility for the human machine to heal itself. Successive generations have been dumbed down and believe that others know best. We think we must intervene and ply it with something that will fix it, but we've lost sight of what the human machine is capable of when the right approaches are used. One never knows what one can achieve unless they continue to push forward, challenge the status quo, and never ever limit themselves or listen to naysayers.

The way I choose to live my life takes much work to maintain – emotionally, physically, and mentally. However, it is incredible to see what I have been able to achieve, and I continue to forge ahead – not knowing what is possible but enjoying every minute of unravelling the human machine in which I inhabit. This approach to my personal life fits perfectly with my professional role. I continue to push boundaries and stretch myself personally, professionally, and emotionally just to see where I am, and then look after myself and do what is necessary to stay in sync.

4

I find that the morning coffee sitting on the bay window out the front, immersed in nature, trees, and birdsong before daybreak has dawned, to be integral to it all.

A significant, major change is that I do not become involved in problems or drama of others and have significantly reduced the types of conversations I have with people – professionally and personally – and with what I read or view on any form of media. This all used to impact my nervous system and can be detrimental to my health.

I learned that the words I speak and allow from my mouth reverberate and come back to me. Some people call it the law of attraction, others call it spirituality. I am not of the latter but firmly believe in collective consciousness and found that when I only speak positively and verbalise what I want to achieve – regardless of what is hammering me both inside and in my life – eventually it starts to turn around. I am not denying what's going on – I am focusing on what I want to create. We are not taught this stuff, sadly, and it took me a long time to work it out. But work it out I have, and the results I now attain are nothing short of incredible.

5

Born a change agent, I have lived my life through this lens. My life's work has been unravelling who I am, and learning and developing at all stages. I am staggered at what I have been able to achieve personally and professionally. It is remarkable, and I continue to push the boundaries in this area. I am grateful for the many opportunities I have had and that I was born in Australia where all of this has been possible.

6

My primary goal when I became an independent consultant was to build an international business, develop my own business model, deliver services to executives globally and to write and contribute to the global media. This has all been achieved. Morphing into many areas since that time – but always under the umbrella of leadership – I have learned that the systems and processes approach that I developed is as effective in an individual's life as it is in their professional capacity and to the organisation. Hence, the inner leadership articles, books, and media conversations commenced.

Determined to disseminate this information globally,
I designed a personal development model. Its purpose:

TO ASSIST EVERY PERSON ON THIS PLANET WITH THE ABILITY TO DEVELOP THEIR INNER LEADER AND TO LIVE THEIR LIFE THROUGH A THOUGHT LEADER LENS.

This is why I am committed to what I do, to sharing my
knowledge globally, and always moving forward in a
positive direction. This is why I feel so passionate and
enthusiastic about what I do; there is never a limit as
to what can be achieved by society, by community,
and by every individual. This is why I fought so hard
to regain my health and to never, ever allow anyone to
determine my future.

There is not one potential.

Potential is determined by you and me and by the society in which we live.

Which, of course, is linked globally.

BOOKS

If it's to be: It's up to me

Back from Hell

Sex in the Boardroom

Thought Leadership

8

1
BURNOUT

Everything on the outside seemed fine.
My confidence and enthusiasm remained
and I could still function as 'normal'.

I was positive, and my mind was swift.

But it was not like that on the inside and had not been
for a long time. I felt that I was close to the breaking
point, a bit like *Humpty Dumpty* – ready to fall off my
perch and crack into many pieces. I could not continue
to pretend. It had got to the point where this was just
about impossible.

It became increasingly difficult to cope with everyday
issues. Things I used to manage easily became difficult
or impossible to do. Each time I felt a little better and
tried to return to my normal pace I would collapse in
a heap, hardly able to function, and have to rest again
for days before starting the process all over again.

I struggled and fought it for a long time until I finally
realised that I needed help. I didn't know what was

happening, and had I known what the initial period was going to be like I would have been less than impressed. Up down; up down: one minute feeling fine, the next horrible. If I was to recover, I knew that I needed to take full responsibility for my health and wellbeing and to think long and hard about anything I did before embarking on possible 'cures'.

There is no shortage of advice available and I had to be careful whose I took, because, when you are as ill as I was, quick fixes can sound appealing. It would have been easy to do whatever anyone said because of how I felt, but then I would have to live with the long-term consequences. I was only interested in a long-term solution. Not willing to take drugs (licit or otherwise), I needed to find out what was going on, accept that what I was doing was not working, and develop a strategic plan that would help me to regain my health.

My first port of call was to speak to one of my health practitioners. This meeting was not useful and I was given a label to contemplate.

12

I WAS NOT WILLING TO ACCEPT THIS AND OVER TIME IT BECAME CLEAR TO ME THAT I WAS BURNT OUT – MY BODY HAD HAD ENOUGH OF BEING PUSHED FOR YEARS ON EMPTY AND WAS NOW REBELLING. I HAD NOT SEEN THE 'EMPTY LIGHT', AND EVEN WHEN I DID, I'D IGNORED IT.

13

Burnout did not happen to me overnight – it was built-up over many years. I knew when I started my business that I was exhausted, but that was too bad because it was just for me and I was not going to allow the opportunity to pass me by.

And, of course, burnout is not just about me.

As a professional working in the area of leadership
I have confidential conversations with all levels of
leaders and employees and I am privy to information
that most others are not – like a *fly on the wall*. I see
leaders and employees regularly either burnt out or
close to it and who have no idea what is happening to
them. They may be aware that they feel unwell, but do
nothing about it. Most just keep pushing themselves
because there is so much to do. I am fairly sure that if
I told them they were showing signs of burnout, they
would simply look at me quizzically. Most would shun
the information; they are as I used to be and do not
want to know about it – they are immortal and running
on adrenalin.

Even if they did accept what I said and consulted a
professional, the chances that they would be asked
about their stress levels, how many hours they work
in a week, what they do to stay healthy, or when they
last went for a long, long holiday uninterrupted by
work are not high. On the contrary, they are likely to be
diagnosed with something else – with one of the many

side-effects of burnout – and treated for that, rather than the underlying issues.

Leaders need to educate themselves and those they lead about the dangers of unchecked stress levels. It is an issue that, if left to fend for itself, will cost industry significantly – the writing is already on the wall. They would also be well advised to include information about burnout in regular staff training and development sessions. While the ramifications of it may initially be ignored or dismissed, if it is spoken about regularly and particularly to those who are at risk, valuable and important information will have been disseminated.

15

Burnout can change a fantastic leader (or anyone) into one who is painful to deal with. They often lose all sight of reality and can become impatient, impertinent, and intolerant. And they can make those who have to associate with them feel ill as well because of all their complaining and whinging. They tend to focus only on the negative aspects of any situation and give an unedited version of the thoughts that are circulating in their mind to anyone who has the unfortunate experience of crossing their path. At times, in their presence, it can feel like being in close proximity to a volcano that is spewing forth inner rot. When in this mode, it is unsurprising that their colleagues are likely to be too scared to tell them that they are not operating as before and try to help them to work out what is happening - it is all swept under the rug and expected to rectify itself. The afflicted often wonder why colleagues who used to be easy to get along with have suddenly become so difficult.

Burnout can be interrupted if the person suffering from it knows what is happening and understands that stress is a normal part of the flight or fight response and that, while we need it to function, has to be managed.

The word needs to get out and burnout needs to be taken seriously.

16

This debilitating disorder does not receive the attention it needs or deserves, is often minimised or scoffed at, thought to occur only to weak-minded individuals. The health problems associated with it can sneak up on us, and it is as though our bodies break down bit by bit. We can try to stitch them up and medicate ourselves in many ways and that is the scary bit: before we know we are ill, we can be very ill.

Many will look for the quick-fix approach and not do their research, which can mask the real issues and they may never be addressed or identified.

We need to stop, learn, and listen and be clear as to what it is – take note as to whether we are already burnt out or too close to the edge.

We all need to be aware of the other health problems associated with it, know not to get *stuck* in any of them, and to know how it can impact anyone who gets in its way.

Back from Hell had been waiting in the wings for years to be written (in an advanced state). It had been worked on often and had a number of titles - those preferred were *High Achiever Syndrome* and *High Achievers.* The people I thought fitted the profile did not recognise themselves and some were offended I had put them into this category at all; they had been taught that being a high achiever was nothing to aspire to.

So much else had occurred throughout this period that the book was at risk of never being finished, but then, 10 months after *Sex in the Boardroom* was published, the push from within came and I knew it was time - the book wanted a voice. While the book may have wanted a voice and while I like to finish what I start – the project became much more than just that, and the book is considerably different from whence it began.

Writing *Back from Hell* has been life-changing; it has enabled me to identify the core issues of my burnout, to put many things into perspective, and has been a catalyst for my recovery. I have learned a lot about me – the good and the behaviour patterns that needed changing. It has enabled me to forge ahead and be clear as to what I can and cannot do at each juncture. Through the process I have gained a respect for what I have achieved, rather than to just dismiss it and to always be focusing on climbing the next summit.

19

The term 'burnout' used in *Back from Hell* does not refer to people who are just tired and cranky, having a bad day, or in need of a good, long rest or holiday. It refers to people who have become ill (physically, emotionally, or mentally) from continuing to push themselves and there is no age that it hits specifically – anyone can get in its way.

2
ADRENALIN KID

For years, I could have been called the 'adrenalin kid'. I'd power along as though I was fuel injected, maintaining 100% productivity. Surging through my body, the adrenalin was like an extra source of energy and fuel. It was wonderful – no wonder people get addicted to it. I felt like I was more than a mere mortal; I was superwoman in action. There were no limits – I was in forward motion. All I'd need was to rest up a bit and off I went again. It gave me courage. Adrenalin was free and licit.

My brain operated like a sports car: thoughts clear, focused, memory brilliant, quick thinking, and continually climbing summits with multiple things on the go at once.

That is until burnout brought me to a screeching halt and the reverse became true.

Ah, the pain of reality. It took a long time before the cracks started to appear, but when they did, it was like a slow leak in a bike tyre. I tried to just patch myself up and get going, but that trickle turned into a waterfall before I knew it and I had to face the cold, hard, brutal truth: something was seriously wrong. I needed to find out what it was.

Before I could understand how such a non-illicit
human resource could compromise my health
and future in the long-term and cause me so many
problems, I felt the need to conduct some research
and identify it from a biological perspective. For our
ancestors, the surge of adrenalin was spent in the
hunt. A period of relaxation followed the hunt, bringing
the body back to a healthy balance. Most people in the
21st century seem to be on a treadmill switched to ten
with little-to-no rest or relaxation on their agenda. Our
bodies are in a state of constant readiness to meet our
challenges because there is just so much to do.

23

Adrenalin flows freely and most of us do not have a
clue as to how, why, or the long-term problems it can
cause. Increased levels of adrenalin in our bodies can
cause a rise in blood pressure and heart rate.
Our muscle tension heightens, breathing rates
increase, and the immune system diminishes. The
affect is cumulative; experiencing more stress means
releasing more adrenalin, overusing the fight or
flight hormone, and we become more likely to get ill

from stress related health problems. Ammon-Wexler works with burnt-out leaders and entrepreneurs and claims that many are seduced by the feeling that adrenalin gives them, but what they're actually doing is enjoying the physiological excitement from an adrenalin high: 'During an adrenalin high your higher thinking centres close down and older, more primitive portions of your brain prepare you for emergency. Over a period of time this leads straight to stage two burnout and serious mental and physical exhaustion' (Ammon-Wexler, 2010).

Ammon-Wexler's long-term studies have identified a number of major factors and three stages that can lead to burnout. The factors are: 'time pressures, excessive responsibility or accountability, lack of adequate support, [and] excessive expectations from yourself or from those you associate with...' (Ammon-Wexler, 2010).

I can relate to some of those factors, yet had no idea how they impacted each other and how they could compromise my health in the long-term. Indeed, I thought I was immune from this because of what else I did to stay well. It took me many wake-up calls before I finally understood that I am the same as anyone else and I do have a limit.

Stress arousal stage: The first stage of burnout is the stress arousal stage. Symptoms include: '...irritable, anxious or forgetful, difficulty with your mental focus, flare-ups of high blood pressure, bruxism (grinding teeth during sleep), insomnia, headaches and acute gastrointestinal distress' (Ammon-Wexler, 2010).

From my perspective, these health problems are so commonplace in developed countries that most of us would not even bat an eyelid if a colleague told us they were suffering from any or all of them.

The low energy stage: As the downward spiral continues, the body tries to maintain its equanimity and, if the cycle of burnout has not been broken at this point, further deterioration will occur. Ammon-

25

Wexler states that the body is trying to cope with mental and physical exhaustion and 'is shifting into conservation mode' (2010). She says that symptoms often include: 'forgetfulness, serious inability to focus, a tendency to procrastinate, excessive time off from work, lack of interest in your work or business, loss of hope and enthusiasm, decreased desire for intimacy and a persistent feeling of tiredness or exhaustion. Other common signs include: social withdrawal from friends and family, cynicism, resentment, apathy and increased substance use – nicotine, caffeine, alcohol or prescription drugs' (Ammon-Wexler, 2010).

The acute exhaustion stage: I experienced some symptoms from each stage that Ammon-Wexler describes and spent far more time in the acute exhaustion stage than I would like to admit to. Some of the symptoms identified by Ammon-Wexler in this stage include: 'chronic sadness or depression, chronic stomach or bowel problems, chronic mental fatigue, chronic physical fatigue, chronic headaches or migraines, difficulty reading or understanding communications and almost total inability to focus. Other common signs may include: a desire to drop out of society, quit work, or abandon one's business or profession and the desire to avoid family, friends, and social situations' (Ammon-Wexler, 2010).

By the time I arrived at this point, I was aware that I was really ill. I did not know what was wrong or how to fix it, but had no intention of staying there.

27

One of the reasons I did not come crashing down sooner than I would have under normal circumstances is because of my long-term commitment to being healthy. I did all the right things (well, most of them) and they certainly held me in good stead; I exercise regularly, have the blood pressure of a teenager, keep myself slim, eat excellent food, and have been committed to traditional health practises for a long time. What I found confusing and difficult to come to terms with was the fact that, while regular medical tests confirmed my excellent health (even in the acute exhaustion stage), I was still experiencing some of the health issues Ammon-Wexler describes. Seeing the information in print and divided into stages made a huge difference to me. It wasn't just me. There were many others who have had similar experiences and there was something that could be done about it.

It would have been easy to become stuck in any of the stages of burnout and then live my life according to that prescription. I could have accepted any one of a number of labels rather than be annoyed with myself for not having listened to my body years ago and be determined that it was a short-term nuisance and do whatever was required to regain my health.

I HAVE SEEN FAR TOO MANY PEOPLE ACCEPT LABELS WITHOUT QUESTION OR GOING FOR A SECOND, THIRD, FOURTH, FIFTH OPINION, OR TRY OTHER WAYS TO RECOVER OR TAKE FULL RESPONSIBILITY FOR THE HEALTH ISSUES THEY ARE CONFRONTED WITH.

29

It is horrible to witness when people do not fight for the equanimity of their life.

I shake my head in disbelief and wonder why anyone would accept another person's diagnosis and go on to live their life under that umbrella.

No matter how clever, kind, or accomplished a professional is or what side of the fence they are from, they only have their knowledge, experience, and education to go from, and whatever information they disseminate is from their perspective and only accurate at the time.

The world is full of *other* professionals who view things differently and who have studied in other areas.

The labels I was staring at had absolutely no appeal to me.

I was not willing to accept anyone else's diagnosis of what my future looked like.

It is also important to note that the current theoretical perspective is just that and science is always looking for new ways of doing things. Who knows what will be discovered tomorrow, next year, next decade, and it is in one's best interest to keep up to date with research so that when discoveries are made we can adjust our thinking and behaviour and approach to life.

It took me 13 long years to find one of my family's health practitioners who changed the course of our history. It was a long frustrating search that cost me significant sums of money on other professionals who were not helpful. I am so glad I continued to look because of the difference he has made not just to me but to the many I have referred him to. I cannot describe how important and valuable he has been and I will always be grateful to him. Thus, I know just how important it is to keep searching until you find what you want and to know that there is a huge amount you can do for yourself.

Each time I have been to one of these brilliant professionals, I have gratefully added more knowledge to my repertoire.

Therefore, it never entered my head at any time during this period to not continue searching for other

available options, or to ever give up before I found the help that I wanted and was right for me.

While I do not stand on tall buildings with my superwoman costume any more, advocating that people become addicted to adrenalin in order to achieve great things in their life and push themselves so hard that they burnout, I do *not* advocate the opposite. Do not take a backseat to your life and just mosey along, spending years procrastinating and not achieving anything of significant value. Do not simply follow other people's agendas, do what previous generations expect, or help other people to achieve their objectives and aspirations while you and your aspirations are left abandoned.

32

Not being aware of the downside of adrenalin enabled me to continue to forge ahead and attain any level I wanted. I never had (and still don't) understand the principle that you can't do anything you want if you are realistic with your expectations and willing to put the necessary hard work into it, monitor your success,

and change what is not working and keep pushing
ahead. This way of living has been normal for me,
and once my confidence was at a certain level I knew
I could continue to achieve what I wanted if I was
tenacious and willing to go without many other things.
People are amazed at my natural drive and what I have
achieved, but there is absolutely no secret to any of it.
Coupled with my then-mate 'adrenalin', I worked hard
and had no intention of slowing down until I got to
where I was headed.

33

The more I get to know myself and the more honest
I am when things are not working and do something
about it, the easier it is for me to maintain functionality.
Modifying my modus operandi was not easy because
this pace was entrenched, and I loved it. This period
has taught me that adrenalin is a normal biological
component in human beings, and without it many of
our forebears would not have survived; they would not
have had the agility or quickness of mind to remove
themselves from danger. However, many of us end
up with adrenalin operating all the time because we

have not been educated and do not understand it, how it works, or the negative aspects to it. We do not balance the mental energy with that of our physical requirements.

I now know when the adrenalin is running; it feels horrible and I know exactly what I have to do to stop it within a short period of time.

This technique works every single time.

34

I cannot go back into the past and change anything, and I am tired of giving myself a hard time for what I did not do or should have done. It serves no purpose other than to make me feel guilty and locked into negative behaviour patterns. I would much rather just take responsibility, get on with it, and ensure that it does not happen again. Now that I know the negative impact adrenalin can have, I will give it the respect it deserves. I can share this information with clients and mention it in articles I write and in media interviews.

3
BLACK HOLES

Wheeler states that a 'black hole is a region of space where the pull of gravity is so strong that nothing can escape from it' (Darling 2003, p56). This analogy describes how I felt in the initial stages of burnout, when I did not understand what was happening or how to get out. In this chapter, I discuss some of the issues I had to contend with before I knew what to do to regain my health. The term 'black hole' is a metaphor and not a label given by any professional. It is the terminology I chose to use because it made sense to me after reading Wheeler's definition and enabled me to think about what was occurring in my life in another way.

Exhaustion and fatigue were nothing new to me. I am like most adults, and in that mid part of your life when there is a lot to do, busy and frantic can become the norm. While I had pushed myself to the limit my entire adult life, there came a point when my body refused to cooperate. I could push myself no more. An overload of stress from extending my body beyond its capacity year after year - physically, emotionally, and mentally – finally caught up and I crashed and burnt out. *How could I possibly achieve my objectives in this state? What on earth was going on? Why did I feel so revolting? Why didn't I bounce back as I always had? Why wasn't what I had done for years working anymore?* These were the questions that troubled me.

I could do much less than I normally did, and at times I could do nothing except lay in bed and just wait for my energy to return. It was as though I was drowning in a dark quagmire of emotions. I had not been there before, and it was not somewhere I wanted to stay. The clothes dryer analogy best describes this experience; my emotions and brain seemed like they were doing somersaults. It seemed dark inside, and I was locked into this state for weeks before I started to feel better. Whatever I seemed to do, I kept falling back into the black holes and when I was out of one it was not over immediately - there was quite a recovery period involved. In the acute exhaustion stage, by the time I had recovered from one, I was often head first into another.

Forever.

I would have learned what I needed to know and just move on.

In order to achieve this, it was essential that I understood what they were; the reasons behind them, the impact they had on me, and what was needed to firstly get out of them and then to stay out. As I understood more and my recovery progressed, the next step from my perspective was to become aware of when I first went into a black hole. I had discovered a couple of things that made a difference while in one, and I wanted to be able to implement the strategies immediately and see how they would impact on the duration and intensity of the black holes.

39

It took a long time for me to gain this knowledge, but when it came it was such a wonderful, magical moment that I will never forget it. I was sitting in the Hilton hotel writing this book and having a coffee. The Hilton hotel has been one of my favourite locations for years and I am a regular visitor. In the acute exhaustion stage, it was one of my safe havens. I could go there when I felt too ill to speak to people, have a coffee or a meal, enjoy the beautiful vista, work if I could or simply read the paper, and enjoy the ambience and down to earth staff.

Even though having just gone into a black hole was not pleasant, to me this was a eureka moment. For the first time I was aware that I was going into one within a couple of hours. I did what I knew worked, and the duration and intensity of the black hole was significantly reduced, lasting days instead of weeks. This moment felt like it was key to my recovery and I felt sure that this knowledge would help me to get out of the acute exhaustion stage and build some resilience. The problem with black holes is that they can happen at any time; they appear to come out of left field and it seems to be the suddenness of a situation that causes them.

40

It is as though when old stuff is meeting new stuff,
it curdles.

It was clear that I had to reduce my workload and I
decided to take it easy for the rest of the year. A few
months later, I had another heart-to-heart with myself
and realised that, while I had reduced my workload, I
was still exhausted. Obviously, I needed to reduce my
workload even further and so I did. I then held myself
accountable to ensure that the rest of the year was
indeed easy and it was. This was a turning point and
made a huge difference – I recovered significantly in
this period. While I still struggled with not being up to
par, I knew it was far better for me to take it easy for as
long as I needed and to fully recover rather than to be
ill and incapacitated for the rest of my life.

41

As an extrovert I must have been standing in the
wrong line when my genetic gifts were handed out.
They have appeared in strange places given that an

extrovert is outgoing and wants to be with people. A consultant and writer are solo professions in many ways. Given that I was limited by what I could do when in a black hole, I had to conserve my energy for my business and clients – friends and other activities had to be put on hold. I found that during this time, I reacted far more than I would like, and noted that some of the self-destructive personal behaviour patterns (habits) I had dealt with years ago resurfaced. I could see how they might damage good relationships if I did not take time out and I did not want this to occur because the friendships were far too important and I know just how long it takes to make good friends.

It was best at this juncture to just stop and wait for things to improve, however it took a lot longer than I expected and the social isolation made everything significantly worse.

It was cruel.

The situation required me – and only me – to take absolute control. I *had* to find the way. Conduct research. Note findings. Evaluate over and over again. Process it in my mind over and over again and not allow myself to get stuck at any point. It was a trial-and-error approach – a pragmatic approach. I had to search for the *right* professionals who could help me help myself. I had to be completely honest with myself, change what was not working, continue to refine my learnings.

I had to work out what was causing me to fall back into black holes and be ill for so long.

43

I had to adhere to what I thought would take me to the next level. Initially – with little or no clarity. This only occurred as I clawed my health back – inch by inch, moment by moment, bit by bit, day by day, week by week, month by month, year by year.

I had to be hard headed.

I had no intention of ending up on a scrap-heap or not being able to achieve what was important to me. Having achieved far more professional and personal goals than I ever thought possible, every day was potentially a new beginning.

Enacting my natural stubbornness, determination, positive frame of mind, knowledge that no one has all the answers, and my never, ever give up attitude, an absolute commitment to me was what had to occur.

44

My belief that I would not stop until I had made a full recovery was what pulled me through.

It was necessary for me to alienate anyone who dragged me down or who wanted more from me than I could give. When you are ill, the parasites can come out to play; only interested in their own needs – not giving one thought as to how the other person is feeling or what their needs are.

Hindsight being the erudite teacher, it is clear that, had I been waiting for a miracle or luck to intervene, I would still be waiting and all of the incredible next steps that I have achieved would not have occurred. I would not be in sync again. I would not be achieving my goals or writing or challenging the status quo in a myriad of ways. If life was as simple as those who use platitudes, why would anyone bother doing anything? Rather than never, ever giving up when life is throwing difficult situations at us, we might just as well sit on a rocking chair on the porch, wait for the saviour to rock up, sip on a Chardonnay, and let it all unfold.

45

4

WHOSE AGENDA

Encased in our mother's womb we are safe, warm, protected, and live in this beautiful environment for the period of our gestation – our first home and experience. We are affected by our mother's decisions; by what she eats, how she lives, and her emotional state; all of which have in turn been influenced by her life, DNA, and environment. When the time is right, we are born and we venture into this – our new world. We are completely dependent on those who care for us and are impacted by all who are in our life. It will be a long time before we can articulate our needs, and we will consider whatever occurs in this period to be *normal* because we do not have anything to compare it with or the maturity to do so. It will be years before we can gauge just how functional our upbringing really was.

As advanced as we *think* we are in the 21st century I note that no formal or informal education is required to be a parent. For many, kids just arrive and while it is such an exciting time, the reality hits new parents hard – this is a hard gig. We do it the best way we can and

47

it is a steep learning curve. Unless we actively pursue education, we will be driven by how we are feeling at that particular moment and how we were raised because that's all we know. As parents we expect kids to do what they are told because we believe we know best. This continues in most aspects of a child's life: at home, extended family, friends, and school. It is a brave kid who challenges this wisdom and there's generally a high price for those who dare. Some adults will relish a young person's inquisitiveness and courage, but most don't; they think they are being rude and should be taught respect. Kids don't have a choice at this point – they *have* to listen to those who are in authority because they depend on them for their very survival. All they can do is act out, and when they do it is mostly met with disapproval and punishment.

We are told many things by our parents, family, school, media, and authority figures. Some of it is useful, other not so but it is always from the other person's perspective: their agenda. It is in the best interest of the *other* that we do exactly what we are told – it makes their life easier. We learn from a tender age that it is best not to rock the boat or argue because it will make our life easier; we will spend less time on the naughty chair, in time out, in cold corridors, being suspended from school, or rejected by our peers and others for not conforming to their expectations regardless of whether or not they were realistic or right for us in the first place.

School comes and most kids can't wait to get there – they'll have lots of friends to play with and new things to learn. As they progress through school, kids learn many other things in addition to what was on the curriculum. There are great kids to play with and there are bullies – those who taunt them. Even if there isn't much wrong, kids will find something to tease them about. While this is just kids' stuff, I know from experience and having worked with many people that the school yard stuff has an impact on us for the rest of our lives and I have noticed that much of this behaviour marches straight into the workplace. Our

49

childhood and school experience define who we become as adults.

Adolescence is a time of great change for a young person in every single area of their life. It is necessary for youth to find their own feet otherwise they will be clones of their parents – they need to challenge authority and their parent's rules. The changes in their brain are unparalleled, yet most of us have no idea about this. It is not widely known that the adult brain is not formed until we are 26 years of age and I regularly see toddlers, children, and adolescents expected to behave and think like rational adults – a thing that even adults find difficult to do.

In addition to leadership development, I have also worked with kids in a number of capacities throughout my adult life. Not that long after becoming an independent consultant, I had the privilege of being part of a youth mentoring pilot project. The goal was to improve student engagement in learning, to increase retention rates to complete schooling, and to support students with the transition from primary school to high school. The state government, as part of its social inclusion agenda, provided funding. The project connected schools, government, businesses, and communities. Over 100 mentors were assigned to work with a young person and their commitment was expected to be for a minimum of 12 months. It was the first time a youth mentoring project like this had been trialled with kids of this age in my home state.

Interestingly, when speaking to a colleague who had worked with hundreds of youths about this pilot project, I was informed that it would not be successful because the kids were too young – that mentoring was better with youth in upper high school. The outcomes of the project did not support this statement: in fact, the reverse became true. It was phenomenal to see the changes that occurred and it was not only the youth who benefitted – every single person involved gained a huge amount and it was a delight to be part of it. The project became so popular that a number of children put their name down on a waiting list because they

51

had seen how much the other kids loved having their mentor. One gorgeous young child waited for over 12 months and regularly asked when she could have a mentor. When she was allotted her very own mentor, they developed a great rapport and did all sorts of interesting things together. This little love was full of energy and enthusiasm and ended up leading school assemblies and having many kids who wanted to be her friend. Another lovely young adolescent ended up becoming a role model for his peer group, and along the track he gained employment, purchased a car, and reviewed and changed certain aspects of his life.

52

A clinical psychologist I met during this period and whom I admire greatly for the work he does with adolescents is Andrew Fuller. He has been working with youth for years. He facilitated a workshop for the program and one of the things Andrew said during his presentation was, *'in fact someone probably should put a sign on the frontal lobes of most early adolescents saying* "closed for construction"*'* (Fuller, A 2006, pers. comm.). The workshop was valuable and reminded participants that we need to be tolerant and understanding of kids at this age and not expect them to behave like adults when they are transitioning from adolescence to the next stage.

And when the next stage does arrive: finally, we made it – we are adults. Life will be rosy and wonderful for evermore. *But* there is a problem with this belief – no one had warned us that life is not always going to be one long, beautiful holiday. We find (at times) that it is a hard slog and emotions and people are hard to deal with. Our rose-coloured-glasses vision of the world is often challenged. Most of us wonder what on earth is going on and the 20s and 30s can be a tough time. We think it must be just us because the surface view of those around us is that they all have a great life. We often do not share this inner secret with anyone because we do not want to be sprung – our secret being revealed that we are lesser.

53

If we take full responsibility for our personal development and life, and work with professionals who can help us to achieve our goals, it is often seen by others (and us until we know better and know that it is just another myth we have believed) as a retrograde step, whereas in reality the opposite is true.

There are those who will tell us that seeking help is a remedial step and why waste your money. *You don't need to do that. I can help you. You are doing what with those professionals? Can't you handle your problems by yourself? You are too sensitive. You worry too much. You think too much.* A whole raft of advice and platitudes are rolled out and thrown at us and the words: *just get on with it,* are heard often. This does nothing for one's confidence or self-esteem and it can stop us from searching for answers because we think we should be able to do it by ourselves, and if we can't then we must be losers.

54

Working with a mentor or professional who provides us with guidance, support, encouragement, and a clear vision forward, who is well educated and trained in their area of expertise, and who has significant runs on the board is one of the most important, positive, and liberating things we can ever do in our lifetime. They can provide much needed assistance – tell us what we should have been told years ago. If they do not just simply talk about the problem and tell us what we should do but instead are forward thinking and help us to unravel our lives, they can be brilliant. There is no doubt that this can stop us from getting stuck and wasting valuable years of our life.

55

THE MORE I STAND BACK AND LEARN ABOUT AGENDAS - WHOSE THEY ARE, AND THE IMPACT THEY HAVE ON ME - AND THINK CLEARLY BEFORE DECIDING WHAT ROAD I WILL TAKE, THE MORE MY QUALITY OF LIFE INCREASES AND THE MORE I DO WHAT IS RIGHT FOR ME. BECOMING AWARE AS TO JUST HOW MUCH I HAVE BEEN (AND STILL AM) INFLUENCED BY OTHER PEOPLE THROUGHOUT EVERY SINGLE STAGE OF MY LIFE AND HOW THIS HAS SHAPED THE DECISIONS I HAVE MADE, THE LIFE I HAVE LED AND THE PERSON I AM HAS ASTOUNDED ME.

I will never know all the agendas that have impacted
me because I am not privy to that level of detail and
do not have time to analyse every situation that I've
ever been in. I am at a point in my life where I feel that
I have a sense of control and believe that I can make
informed decisions on most things. I know that if I want
to live my life my way then every time someone gives
me their opinion it is essential to think about what has
been said, and either toss that advice aside or review
it and make an informed decision as to what part I will
implement. Having the confidence and courage to do
this has taken years; it is still not easy and the ability to
do so is very much impacted by my stress levels.

57

There are some strong characters in the world
determined to dominate and badger until the other
person does as they say, whereas in fact they would
be wise to turn the spotlight inward and work on their
own stuff instead of telling others how to live their life.
This is why I love the process I use with clients. It does
not dictate what they should do. Rather, over time,
it gives them the confidence and clarity to work out

what they need to do in order to achieve their desired outcome and develop their own way forward. It is always a delight to see their confidence increase and to be part of the process and their experience.

This chapter has outlined my thoughts and experiences on what agendas are and how they can influence us at every stage of our life. It has reminded me how important it is not just to follow the leader but to be one, and to ensure that we take full responsibility for every decision we make and action we create. We do not want to live our life as though we are on a leash and feel that we have to do what we are told or suffer the consequences. We want to give our self the best chance of living our life according to our own values and principles.

58

5
THE FIRST CLIENT'S STORY

The next two chapters are from past clients I worked with shortly after becoming an independent consultant. Though I no longer work in this area and these women are no longer clients, they have given me permission to share their stories. They are remarkable women and it was a pleasure and privilege to be able to stand alongside them while they reclaimed their life.

This first client read an article I had published in a newspaper and as soon as she saw it, she knew it was for her. She rang, made an appointment, and we commenced working together the next day. In her early 30s she was a manager, married, mother of two young children, and an equestrian who managed a farm along with her husband. She came to me desperate to find out why she could no longer ride her beloved horse. The previous 12 months had been a nightmare for her; she had been struggling with stress and anxiety and it had destroyed her quality of life. This chapter is in the client's own words, outlining many insights about what was happening in her life and what she needed to do in order to regain a sense of control. It was not that she had an incurable anxiety disorder – which was confirmed by her medical practitioner – rather it was that she could not physically, emotionally, or mentally sustain her workload and commitments.

Who am I?

This is a hard question.

I am a fun-loving person who wants the best for everyone around me. I am positive and interested in others. I like to work hard and to excel and do not like listening to people complain about their life when they are not prepared to make changes. I have little tolerance for people who are not prepared to help themselves. While I don't expect anything from people other than honesty, I know that I set high standards for myself. Determined to succeed, I know I am a great friend.

Where am I?

That is a hard question.

I am at a great stage in my life where I am young enough to evaluate and make positive changes. I live on a dream property with the horses in the backyard. This is something I have longed for. My children are doing well; their perception of life inspires me. They have no inhibitions and will give anything a try. My oldest son sometimes worries me; he suffers from mild anxiety. I can see it already but it doesn't stop him from doing anything. I have a fantastic husband who loves me dearly and we are moving on the same path. We have grown together more this year than ever.

I have been aware of anxiety like never before, which has been a real eye-opener to me, but it is where I am and I am dealing with it. The future excites me because my thought patterns are changing.

I didn't realise how much I was fuelling my own anxiety.

I am on the road to recovery. I don't know where I'm heading but it's a great place and I am becoming a greater me.

If I go back to October of last year, I remember the morning my employer rang me asking me to return to my place of work – all I could think of was joy. I had been off from work on maternity leave and it was good for my self-esteem to be wanted back. Now I look back and think it was just a solution to money troubles we were having at the time. It justified the large sum of money I spent on my kitchen, it made life easier on the farm, and it took the load off my husband. To me this all felt good – not to mention the fact that someone was acknowledging me for my skills and previous achievements.

After three months of slogging away, guessing my way through most of the problems, I found myself back in the same old job I had held several years before.

Whenever anyone saw me, I was asked to solve another problem.

Everyone was happy with what I could do, except me.

When my manager created my three-month task list I just crumbled. Not only was it an impossible ask, it was unrealistic to expect anyone to be able to do this in 18 hours per week.

65

Before I knew it, I started to experience dizzy spells. The first one was on a shopping day out with a girlfriend. I seriously thought there was something drastically wrong with me.

After that experience I became afraid of so many things.

I felt constantly overwhelmed.

I was not able to see the light at the end of any tunnel and felt my life was collapsing and that there had to be something physically wrong with me.

Several more of these dizzy spells and I was convinced.

Anxiety

What does anxiety mean to me?

Anxiety to me is when I have so much to deal with and so much to achieve that I struggle trying to give everything my all.

What is it about?

It is a state of mind where other things are controlling me.

Anxiety is worrying about outcomes.

It tends to consume me.

How does it affect me?

At home I tend to lose patience with the kids. I get tired and worn out. I worry [about] why things aren't the way I want them when I give so much.

I can become critical when I am anxious; I suppose it gets the attention off me.

I don't think clearly when I am anxious.

At work, I tend to feel isolated when I am in this state and often wish I worked in a larger company where there is a bigger team to share the load because I have to control everything from staff to financials. I am good at what I do, but I am convinced not one of the three partners is aware of the pressure they put on me.

67

It is their right to have demands, but because I am not running one business but three that operate under the one roof I get very stressed.

How does it impact on my life?

Anxiety has really impacted me over the past 12 months.

The feeling I woke up to every morning was one of desperation.

Trying so hard to keep everyone happy and impressed with me, I had lost every ounce of determination and courage that I had ever had. How sad. I wasted a whole year of my life. I will never get that time [back] again. I hope my family hasn't suffered too much. My return to my employment has tested everything I have.

My life always seems so fantastic to others.

Look what you've got - look what you've achieved -
you are so lucky.

I am not lucky.

Neither my husband nor I have ever been given anything.
We just simply believe we are capable of almost
anything and work hard to get it. We are a good team.

The saddest thing about the impact anxiety has had
on my life recently has been the physical impact.
I've had dizzy spells (not in the last three months,
but the six prior to that), back and neck pain,
headaches, along with other health issues.

69

What started to make me more aware of this was
when I would walk on my property and say to myself
'I am safe'.

I felt like the world was not a safe and happy place
to be in.

My sanctuary is at home with my family and animals. I am glad I have got this.

When wasn't I anxious in my life?

There have been so many things to cause me anxiety. Being in business for us has been stressful. My husband and I have had the business since I was 19 years old. We have gained a tremendous amount from having a business, but you never really are free of it. My husband has had four weeks off in nearly 15 years. [Of that,] we spent the first nine days together in our married life back in April of this year – we have been married nearly 14 years.

I haven't been anxious all that time.
In fact, I have been extremely happy.

My anxiety doesn't destroy my outside world,
only the inside one.

I think, probably, when my son was a baby and I was home for a year being a mum, breastfeeding, enjoying this new wonder in my life was probably when I wasn't anxious.

Reasons for anxiety one day this week

Tuesday was a shocking day.

The pace of synchronising everything did take its toll. The day did go to plan extremely well, apart from the hold-up at work. I like being flexible and flitting from one thing to another, but I felt my stress levels were certainly up.

I had no tolerance for inconveniences – not a good attitude for my staff but they need to know when to bring things up and when not to. After the day I did reflect and question whether I could have handled things better.

71

I don't think you can do so much in one day and not have a reasonable amount of stress. I am always open to suggestions.

The good thing about my day on Wednesday was that my time with my horse was extra special. There was no stress or anxiety. I am proud of where I am with him. I do need to get on him soon and I am looking forward to it at last.

72

When am I not anxious now?

I am no longer anxious around my horse (this will be tested when I start to ride again), when I am at home with my husband, or when I am at home for my days off. Likewise, I am not anxious when I walk, have a massage, or when I am out in the garden. I love being home on my own. I do enjoy my own company, but I don't get enough of it.

I am not anxious around my friends unless there is something major happening in the background.

I do not think that anxiety is such a bad thing if you are aware of it as I have become. I do believe it pushes me, but I want to be able to think clearer when I am stressed.

I am so sad that I didn't recognise earlier what was happening to me. I now have a lot of hard work to do to prevent myself from falling back into the same trap.

I have become aware that, when I get anxious, my body responds in a certain way. It is only trying to protect me, but I need to now focus on 'prevention' rather than 'cure'.

One step forward

On the weekend I was hanging up some baskets on my veranda posts. Because I am not that tall it was almost impossible. For the first time in a long time I said to myself 'I am determined to do this' and I did.

When I heard myself say that, I almost cried.

73

That's what has been missing – my determination. How vulnerable I felt without it. I can't make clear or precise decisions without it.

For 12 months, every time I have had to make a decision, I have felt confusion. My thoughts have been so fuzzy – there hasn't been any clarity whatsoever.

Where to from here?

The future is going to be fantastic.

74

My husband and I are starting new ventures, both doing what we do best. We are providing a service, the overheads are going to be relatively low and I just have this amazing feeling of peace that everything will be fine.

I have never felt this inner belief and confidence before.

This would have really scared me six months ago because of the "what if's". I can honestly say they aren't even going to be an issue. We will be fine and our future is going to be just great. In some ways I am content with what has happened in the last year because it allowed me to seek help and the answers have come thick and fast.

Once again, it hasn't been all easy.

What I know now

I would never have known that behind my fear of riding was just an anxious, stressed-out girl who needed a break. What would have happened if I hadn't had the courage to contact Merydith and work with her? I don't know? I went to Merydith because of work related issues and had absolutely no idea what was really underpinning the anxiety. All I thought was wrong with me was that I had become afraid to ride.

It wasn't that at all – my stress levels were so high I could not function properly and I was burnt out.

As I have taken the pressure off myself, I can see things differently.

Everything became a challenge and added to my stress levels.

I can now relate this to many areas of my life. Never again will I put myself in that position of fear and anxiety. I should have recognised it sooner, but I didn't and I have paid a really heavy price for it.

I do not ever want to feel physically ill from worry again.

It has run my life for 12 months and taken away my courage, my power, and my determination.

I have felt weak and helpless in every area of my life and now must begin a healing process. I have resigned from the job because, through the work with Merydith, I realised that I actually hated it and stayed there only because I so desperately wanted to make everyone happy. This was achieved but it was at my expense.

It is important to review what I am doing regularly and examine my thought processes. I am the only one in control of my life and will never give my power away again. I am healing on the inside and starting to believe in myself and, while I want everyone to come with me, I don't think they all will. A couple of my friends are hesitant with my change in thinking and behaviour. I will not hold back just for their sake and will be riding again very soon.

I am looking forward to something, but I am not sure exactly what.

Where to from here?

Up.

77

6
THE SECOND CLIENT'S STORY

A 46-year-old businesswoman had tried many self-help treatments over the years; some had been useful, while others were a complete waste of time and money; this client felt cynical about any further work in that area. She said that she felt dark inside, had no motivation, could visualise herself all bent over and hunched up. She felt that she was in a rut and that there was no way out. From her perspective, the only difference between a rut and a grave was that the rut had the ends kicked out. Her story is painful and sad, but inspiring. One full of courage. The words are her own and identify how, bit-by-bit, she clawed back her life and climbed out of the rut she had been stuck in for years over a period of only six weeks. It was a privilege to work alongside this lovely woman while she did what she needed to do to reclaim her life.

79

Session 1: the session helped me to clarify my personal life a bit more. Another step in a positive direction. One step closer to climbing out of the rut

I am in. I am feeling clearer, have a bit more energy – don't feel so bogged down and have an element of hope. My experiences and personal development over the past six years are providing a benchmark for what I am doing now – almost like a jigsaw really.

Session 2: this session was really good. I am so glad that I found out about the process that Merydith uses. It gives me clarity, hope, and inspiration. Merydith is always so positive and accepts me for who I am. Because of her objective views and discussions, I am beginning to acknowledge just how far I have come through this journey of life. I always feel that I am not doing much and that I could be doing a lot more (the old habit) but the sessions help me to see just how much I am doing and how far forward I have come. Many people seem to be stuck in this mindset, yet are not aware of this. I am aware of where I am and, through this work, I am moving into whatever I choose to do.

That is a huge step in itself.

80

The process is at times challenging and not easy, but I am glad I have made the decision to do it and that I am persisting. It would be so easy to stop, but then I would still be stuck in a rut and I *don't* want that. I am ready for my life to change – and I want to be in the driver's seat this time.

Session 3: we debriefed last week and talked about the workbook entry I had done in relation to 'not being good enough' as a child. This was good for me because, until I started this work, I didn't realise that this was a deep thought of mine. I am now able to see why some things are as they are, acknowledge them, change them, and move on. We talked about 'old habit = perfectionism' and new 'habit = moderation, reality, and acknowledgement'. I am critical towards myself and I don't give myself credit for the hard work I have done. I will change this, and acknowledge and celebrate me.

81

I am still uncertain that I will achieve as much as I want in the sessions remaining, but I am willing to be patient and work hard. I enjoy talking to Merydith in the sessions because they make me feel good about *me* and I haven't felt that for a long time. I see that it's *okay* to feel the emotions I feel. I am there at the moment, but I won't always be. While I am writing this, straight after our session, I am feeling inspiration and hope. There will be a happy and rewarding life for me. I will come to a point where I treat myself with respect again. It is just going to take time, patience and persistence.

82

Each small step I take and acknowledge is one step in the right direction.

I am slowly putting in solid foundations and climbing out of the rut I was in; so **celebrate.**

Session 4: I really enjoy my sessions. They make me see just how far I have come and how much personal development I have done. Because I find it easy and I 'just do it', I assume that everyone does. And I always say 'don't ever assume, because you are usually

wrong'. Well, I was wrong about me. I do a lot of work and I am successful – I just didn't realise it. Today's session was about 'getting it' – start seeing what it is that I am doing and acknowledging each small step (grain of sand) along the way as I gradually build my beach. I feel like I am at last starting to get a sense of direction. By writing in my workbook and listing things I am starting to see the types of things I am good at, that I enjoy, and that I want to learn about.
It is forming a story.

83

I had some great insights this week: awareness of me and how much I am doing; feeling good inside because I am actually doing things – this creates a sense of purpose (the spark that had almost died out). I am now doing things for me, because I want to do them and because I enjoy them. I am starting to take care of me and not looking for someone else to do it. No one else is going to take care of me the way I need it – I have to do it for myself.
The joy has to come from within.

The way this will happen is through this work,
research, personal development, and action.

I need to be aware of my perfectionism.

It is a habit that has been with me for most of my
life so it will take a while to become aware of when
I slip back into this. When I am in this mode, I need
to acknowledge what it is (old habit), then step into
acknowledgement, moderation, reality (new habit)
and look at where I have been and what I have done
and celebrate this – stop looking at what I need to do
or feel that I should be doing. This really is irrelevant.
I need to learn from the past and live in the present.

I did write in my workbook yesterday about the rage
I felt.

It was an extremely intense feeling that I experienced.
At least now I have worked through that and have
peeled one more layer of the onion away.

Session 5: another excellent session. I could feel the 'shift' in the session. We did not need to discuss my emotions quite as much as we have previously because I am in a better state of mind and feeling much happier. Although, having said this, I still need to be aware of not getting bogged down in the emotional stuff. See situations for what they are, analyse them, 'what did I learn?', and move on. The negative emotions just drain my energy.

I found it interesting to learn that I am not the only one who gets bored quickly.

I didn't realise this also happened to other people. Merydith says she has found that many intelligent people also have the same issue to contend with.

It is okay to be bored.

All I have to do is then say 'well, okay, I am bored. Now what can I do about it?' It is okay to change careers if

85

that is what I want. I have been given a lot of options to look at this week in regards to business. [I have] discussed lots of things that I did not know existed.

I need to start thinking about where I will go and what I will do after the initial coaching series. I will return for other sessions, but need to learn how to manage myself and use the sessions to see where I am up to and make a plan for [my] next steps. It is time for me to move out of my comfort zone and start meeting and talking to people who are of a like mind and can offer objective points of view and interesting conversations.

This is only the very beginning of the new me.

I will keep moving forward at a steady pace and continue learning about who I am and what I want in my life.

My days [of] caring for others to a very high degree are in the last five years. I can see light at the end of the tunnel and will still always care and love my family, but once my youngest child finishes school, she won't be quite as dependent on me.

I will have more freedom.

The work I've done with Merydith has given me things to think about and actions to do. Through this, because I am being challenged, I gain excitement and a sense of purpose. I have got something interesting to do.

Session 6: I am out of the rut and this needs to be celebrated.

I have been stuck in a rut for so many years and now, after having worked with Merydith for such a short time, I feel I have actually succeeded in climbing out of the rut I was in.

Wow.

This is incredible and amazing.

Now it is like looking at me and the world with new clarity and direction.

In this session we also spoke about me taking responsibility for where I am now and not focusing on where I will be in five years. I have a clearer understanding of this now and can see the worth of bringing things back to a shorter time frame. A saying I read sums this up: 'my future is created today, not tomorrow'.

88

I have built a solid foundation and now am continually building onto this foundation.

We talked about saying things succinctly so that I get into the power of the event and out of the emotions. Emotions are unbelievably powerful and, if not used in a positive and constructive way, can be damaging.

It is interesting for me now that I am more aware because I can sit back and observe interactions between people. Most are not even aware of the games they play and the different 'hats' they wear depending on who they are interacting with.

I still find it difficult to 'think on my feet'.

I seem to need time to sit with things quietly on my own and think about them before I come up with a reasonable answer.

This is okay – I just need time to process things.

89

Session 7: I am so pleased I had the courage to do this work because I am so much more focused and definitely happier. When I started, most of my days were bad and, while I still have my bad days, that is what they are – it is just a bad day. I look at it for what it is and move on.

Sometimes this is difficult and I find it hard to be objective.

The sessions help me greatly to see what is
happening – the saboteurs and other things that
hold me back. It is then easier to see it for what it is.
It is important that I keep having good days and that
I focus on these and find joy in them. Really look at
the small things that bring joy into my life. There are
heaps when you start looking. When I had a bad day
on Monday, I was able to talk to another mum and see
where she was at with her four children (two under
two-years-old).

90

It made me see how far I have come, how hard
I have worked, and the wonderful position I now
find myself in.

I now have so many opportunities open to me
and I have worked hard to get to this point.

Our sessions are now full of insights and information
(not that they weren't before, I just didn't see them
as clearly) because I am not bogged down in all the

emotions. I am so much happier and clearer. There are still things I would like to change and this will be ongoing for the rest of my life.

It has been about *me* – no one else, just me, and I haven't had to give to others. It really has made me feel better about myself and given me back my power.

It is useful for me to re-read my workbook and my other writings; it helps me re-frame and stay positive on a bad day. Today's session was really enjoyable. I just keep learning so much more about me – learn why I do things, why I enjoy things, why I am who I am.

Session 8: once again I learned more about me. It is so good looking at me and why I do things and not focusing on other members of my family.

I have been a mother and wife since I was 18 and it is great to just think about me and what I want.

We spend most of our lives trying to sort other people's problems out that we forget to address our own.

This week we discussed 'where do I go from here?'

What do I really want to do with my life?

I will do some research into this. I need to be specific and bring it back to the daily things.

What is it that really excites me?

Because my emotions are strong and can dominate, I need to remember to take them out of situations – define it and see it for what it is and then make a decision.

By taking out the emotions, I have more clarity.

Things just are, look at them for what they are.

If you had asked me if I thought I would feel as good
as I do at the conclusion of the initial coaching series
when I first commenced my work with Merydith, there
is no doubt I would have said 'no'.

I honestly did not think this could happen for me
because I was in such a dark place – I felt horrible
and I did not think that anyone could help me escape
from the rut I was in.

To think that Merydith has been able to give me the
tools that have given me hope and a sense of control
over my life in a few short weeks is wonderful.

I can now visualise myself standing up tall,
feeling great.

I have a sense of direction and purpose.

My body feels lighter, brighter – I am taking the next
step in my life.

The process has been fantastic because it has been
all about me.

My whole life has been about caring for others
and now, at 46-years-old, I have finally given to me,
and it feels great.

I will continue to do this because I am important and
I do deserve to be happy and fulfilled.

94

I am at a new beginning and will continue along
this path.

I will never go back to where I was.

There is plenty of support and guidance out there.

I just have to know where to look and ask for help.

I have a lot of inner strength and have done significant other development to have achieved as much as I have in this short time. I am focusing on what I have done and how far I have come and looking at things much more clearly.

7
PERSONAL AUDIT

I have noticed when working with successful organisations that they are not that way by chance. They have a clear plan for their business and regularly refine their systems and processes to see how effective they *really* are. They are not perfect – and they don't try to be – but instead aim for excellence. Having worked in this area for a long time and having seen the benefit of a systems approach within business, it seemed logical for me to teach clients how to transfer these practises into their personal life. However, when I commenced my business, I was surprised to find that this approach was not commonplace.

It seemed to me that the situation occurred largely because we are not taught how important systems and processes are, and those who live their life this way are often laughed at and seen as nerds. It appears that somehow personal success is all 'just going to happen for us, right?' Wrong. In time, when people have a 'let it roll' attitude to life, they can spend years or their whole life feeling as though they are chasing their tail, wishing someone – anyone – would tell them what they should be doing because they sure as heck don't know. It does not have to be like this.

I have listened to hundreds of people wherever I am in the world discuss the amount of time they spend not doing what will bring them the outcomes they want. They talk *only* about their problems and do not know what they actually want to do. Little time (if any) is spent sitting down, taking plenty of time to think about their objectives, researching options, and then getting into action to create their desired outcomes.

98

Conducting a personal audit is not something that has entered their mind and sounds quite weird to them. When I teach clients how to think in a systems and processes manner and then apply those learnings to their professional life it transforms the way they do things and they are delighted with the results attained. When I teach them how to transfer the same skills into their personal life, they are staggered to see just how much difference it makes. It changes the way they operate and increases the success they have significantly in every area of their life and they wish they had known about it years before.

I have watched with interest and excitement and seen how it enables them to turn their life around to a place where they feel successful, empowered, and where they gain much more enjoyment from their life. I then see them tick off achievements, reduce stress levels, improve self-esteem and confidence, and love what they do. They become focused and switched on; they stop the drama, problem thinking, and negative behaviours in their life. They also stop feeling powerless to it.

99

This is not a once-off job, though: it has to be managed all throughout your life.

To ensure that I have the success outlined above, I have found that my personal audit needs to be carried out regularly where time is spent investing in me. This gives me clarity about what I want and what I need to do to ensure it happens. Being by myself, and spending time thinking and reflecting all enables me to become aware and to make necessary adjustments while regularly fine tuning the process. I identify exactly what I *have* to do and become aware of what is important, what is not important, what can be shelved, and what never needs to be done. It is interesting to note that some of what I do can be shelved or delegated and that, when I delegate something, it always brings a smile to my face. When I live like this in all areas of my life, I have far more time to myself because I am always thinking about how I can do what I am doing more effectively. It is the clear, consolidated plan and the execution of said plan that works – and works brilliantly. I know I am limited simply by time and I will be able to do little of what I would like or could do in my lifetime.

100

For many years it seemed logical that I would think in project terms and hold myself accountable until I had achieved whatever it was I was working on. My problem was not that I became lax during this period of burnout, it was simply that I continued to take too much on. I saw many people never finish things. They were enthusiastic in the beginning, but when it took too long or did not go the way they wanted, they lost their passion and gave up. I was absolutely determined never to be party to that type of thinking or behaviour.

Conducting a personal audit is now a simple process, but it has not always been like that. It took a long time to master and to realise just how important and effective it is. It is worth every second; if I do not do it regularly because I think I am too busy, I pay a high price. I end up wasting hours because I can get lost in details and cannot remember where to find things and end up being disorganised. I can feel overwhelmed with responsibilities and my head can spin with what I have to do.

101

For those of us who are committed to conducting our personal audit regularly it sets us apart from the rest and puts us in another league altogether, but sadly most seem to avoid it like the plague because it is seen as a waste of time.

I have felt for a long time that I am in a much better position than even an Olympic athlete because there is only one winner in their race. They train for years to have the opportunity of competing with absolutely no guarantee they will succeed. They go without so much in their life that most of us take for granted and every minute of their day is planned – there is a reason for everything they do. And, at the end of the day, it is brutal – no glory for those who come second, third, or fourth.

I wonder whether anyone takes much time to think about the life of an Olympic athlete, or think that they just get up in the morning, laze around, eat whatever they want, put on their training gear, do little or no training, and win gold. It would be most unlikely that anyone would be this naïve, although most of us have absolutely no idea as to what they go through or without in the time they spend at this level of competition. The work – physical and mental – and the years they devote to their area of expertise is unbelievable and most of us would cringe at the thought. Yet, these athletes know what is required and just how much is involved in every single area of their life if they want to have any chance of success. The reality is: they have very little chance of winning because they are competing with athletes who are just as committed as they are. It is largely determined by their dedication, the people and professionals on

103

their team, their genetic predisposition, their mental acuity, the amount of money their country has to invest in their development, and what they are willing to go without in order to even have the slightest chance of standing on the podium with a gold medal proudly draped around their neck and the beautiful sound of their country's national anthem playing. Technology has enabled coaches of Olympic athletes to monitor just about everything they do – it is big business and highly technical. Countries pride themselves on winning gold – as many as they can – and their success changes the way they are viewed by the rest of the world.

I also know that *my* desire to be successful is only one tiny aspect of the accomplishment. If I sit on a chair and just want it, I will be sitting for a very long time and achieving nothing. My success will not happen overnight. It will probably not happen in the time frame I want at all, but it has much more chance of happening if I am willing to work hard and do what is required to achieve my desired outcomes. I am in a much better position than the Olympic athlete because, if I focus on what is important to me, take the time to conduct a regular personal audit, have the right people on my team, and look after myself properly I can continue to achieve my *gold*.

105

8

HABITS

It has become increasingly clear to me through the work I do and by observing others that most of us dislike change and will avoid it if we can. I am not surprised by this, because from my own experience I know that change is not an easy thing. Any habit I want to change takes time (sometimes a lot of it). It can cause stress and anxiety, requires effort and a serious commitment from me, and can stir up other emotions I would rather have left alone. In all of the time I have spent changing habits, I have never heard anyone talk about the actual process required to change them. Rather, I have only been told to do it – no guidance, no information, just *do it*. When I started changing habits, I did not know what I was doing; I did it because I wanted changes in my life. Over a period of time, I taught myself a process that consistently worked, however it still felt like a walk in the park in the dark most of the time.

When I want to change a habit, it is essential that I take time out to think and clearly identify why I want to change it and what it will be replaced with. I ask

107

myself the following questions: *Will this change give me the long-term success I want? What exactly do I need to do? Who will benefit from it and why? How long will it take? Is it worth the effort? How much difference will it make to my life? Will I stay with the process until I have achieved it? How will I know if I am successful?* Once I have identified that I am changing or implementing a habit for all of the right reasons, I take it to the next level and follow the process closely detailed in my books. While this way of living ensures that I achieve what I want and that I always look to the future, experience has shown that old habits do not want to be given the shove and certainly do not want to acquiesce their power to the 'new kid in town'.

The old one fights for sovereignty.

I find that at the point of transition, when the new habit has become dominant, there is a feeling of confusion in my brain. It can feel as though there is a game of tug of war going on, but I find that if I continue with the new way of operating and don't give in to the old

one's power, that eureka moment I have been waiting for always comes. It is a delight to say the least. It is rewarding when I have that first taste of success because it means my hard work and tenacity has paid off and it encourages me to keep going. At this point in time, I seem to flit back and forth between both habits for quite a while – how long depends on how long the old one has been around and I note there is always a certain level of discomfort with changing a habit – no matter how small it is. At this juncture I have developed a new way of operating I believe is more functional and will hold me in good stead for the future. It gives me the courage to change other habits.

109

But that is not the end of it, there is more.

Even though the new habit is active and I have been practising it for some time, there comes a point when I seem to just stop doing it and return to the old way. The stubbornness and resistance astounds me. It is at this juncture that I need to take charge (once again), discipline myself, be aware that I have slipped back into the old behaviour, and push through that resistance, determined to stay with the new one. This challenge will happen a number of times until the new habit is fully embedded in my brain. Though even then, I must not assume that the old one is gone forever.

110

It would be nice to think this, but the reality is different. From experience, a bad habit can easily become active again if I do not pay attention and regularly reflect on what I am really doing as opposed to what I think I am doing. Allowing stress levels to become high can reactivate old habits that have been dormant for any stretch of time.

This is incredible, but just shows how habits are stored and kept.

The mind is a powerful force and, while I have much more of a handle on it these days, I have not learned how to tame it. Success depends on how I am feeling on any given day, how honest I am with myself and how determined I am not to be dominated by habits that do not serve me well. It doesn't matter whether the habit is large or small or how long I have had it: the same process is required. Without the facts, change can be hard work and can take much longer than expected. We are not told about the inner turmoil it can cause or just how easy it is to revert to old ways of operating.

The more I work with leaders and everyday people and observe human behaviour, the more my eyes are opened. I find that most have never been taught basic principles or how to change habits to ensure success in their professional or personal life. Given that change is fundamental to the human condition and that we will be required to do it countless times throughout our life, this seems like an anomaly.

While many professionals skirt around the edges, they do not lay out the whole process or teach us the method. Their spiel is aimed to motivate us. While that feeling is great while it lasts, when it goes away we are left with what we had before – no skills or way forward. We're often left feeling even more guilty and useless because we have been told we *should* know what to do but don't, and we don't dare ask because everyone else looks as though they know what to do. The high achiever in me has seen me adhere to these totally

unrealistic principles throughout my whole life, and I
have often given myself a hard time for not knowing
how to do something, or for not knowing the answer
even when I'd had no relevant training or development
in the area.

When I went to university to complete an
undergraduate degree as a mature aged student I
had not studied at that level before and hence did not
know what was required of me. In sessions, held to
teach new students how to write an academic paper,
we were told that it was an argument on paper and I
took it literally – I argued and was quite aggressive. It
took me a long time before I knew what the term meant
and you can imagine how embarrassed I felt when I
realised what the term did mean.

Even right at the beginning, I felt that I should be able
to gain a high grade without prior knowledge, but I
learned that it takes much time and effort before this
can be achieved. When I spoke to a successful student
about wanting to receive credits for my papers, she

113

told me that if I wanted to be a distinction student then I needed to hang around with distinction students. I followed this advice. She also advised me to inform my tutor that I wanted to work towards a credit for my papers. When I approached him on this topic he was unable to hide his shock; he arched his eyebrows and his pupils dilated before he could compose himself enough to reply with 'if you want to gain a credit, you will need to improve quite a bit.'

114

I continued to work on this and had a tutor for a subject I was studying as part of a cross-institutional postgraduate degree in education and politics from three major universities ask me whether he could discuss a paper I had recently submitted with his tutorial students. Initially, I was unaware as to whether this request was made because it was so appalling that he wanted to give the students a good laugh and a lesson on not what to do, or whether it was of a high level. He had requested to use my paper because it was a high distinction.

As part of the youth mentoring program that I was involved in, I had the opportunity to regularly speak to mentors who volunteered their time to work with primary school and high school students. Mentors ranged in ages, had a range of occupations, and came from diverse backgrounds. In one of the workshops that I facilitated for the mentors, a business woman in her 40s asked me how to change a habit. She had been told many times to do it throughout her life, though no one had ever explained the basic but critical process to her. She felt ashamed to ask because she thought she should already know. It is always risky when you think you are about to ask a dumb question in a group setting, because you do not know how other participants will react. But, from my experience, those brave ones pave the way for what many others would like to have done yet did not have the courage to do. I went through the complete process with her and felt glad that she had stepped out of her comfort zone and had the courage to ask me.

115

It is one thing to tell someone to change; it is yet another to explain why they need to, how it is done, the reasons behind it, and what they are likely to experience physically, emotionally, and mentally when they do change habits. Had I known the whys and hows about change, it would have made such a difference to my life. I would have understood what was happening and why, and I would've learned that if I followed the bouncing ball then I would be fine. Decades of anxiety, stress, and angst would have been reduced and I could have just got on with it. I could have employed CBT principles and talked myself through each habit change knowing – with confidence – that it would work if I persisted.

I rarely speak to anyone who finds the change process easy.

Certainly, there are those who are as committed to change as I am and who struggle through it as I did, wondering what on earth they are doing. They're

determined not to give up, though *always* possess
a certain level of confusion.

We need to teach people of all ages the exact process
required to change habits, and what is happening in
the brain at the time and why this is so. We need to
teach them to think laterally, to finetune the process
and to work out what suits their temperament. It is not
a 'one size fits' all approach: once they know the basics
of how the change process works, they can modify it to
suit themselves.

117

We could teach people that the resistance they
experience when wanting to do something different is
normal. Instead of fearing change, we can teach them
to embrace change and talk about the possibilities that
it can bring to their lives. We can provide mentoring
and support them until they fully understand what is
involved and how it works.

We could help them through the tough periods so that
they can taste success, feel what it is like, and then,

as they become more confident with their small wins, they can move onto the bigger issues in their lives.

Doing this could change the very fabric of our lives and help change become second nature to all of us rather than something we avoid because we do not understand it.

118

IT WOULD ALSO HAVE A HUGE IMPACT ON SOCIETY AT LARGE AND WE COULD START TEACHING CHILDREN THESE CONCEPTS FROM THE TIME THEY ARE BORN AND THEN RIGHT THROUGHOUT THEIR LIFE.

If we were all taught these basic, incredibly important concepts in palatable bits, it is my firm belief that people would spend far less time in their own personal hell – in black holes – struggling with life.

Knowing how difficult it is to change habits and why this is so has made a huge difference to me. It has enabled me to separate knowledge from emotions and to become aware that, if I am willing to persevere with what I am doing, over time the new way of behaving will become *normal*. However, it is still not easy. Focus is important, as is clarity of mind and making sure that I am doing what I really want – not what I think I should be doing. I always stop and think about any new habit I am about to embark on to ensure it takes me in the direction I want. If it does not, I do not venture forward because I know that, before long, the habit will be normal and I am fully aware as to what is required to change it once it's there.

119

I am pleased I had mastered the process before I went into the downward spiral of burnout, and now I am even more committed to this way of operating.

It is integral to my future.

A client in his mid-30s said that 'it is far better to give a child these skills than to try and fix a broken adult.'

CBT OR CBT1

Even with all of the advances that science has made, no one has been able to replicate the brain or even come close to doing so, and few know how to harness its power and brilliance. To me, the brain is the most remarkable thing I have ever come across. Free and ours just because we are human, it has the ability to heal itself and the agility to create new links when one part of it is unable to function. Once thought to be rigid, it is now known to be malleable. Every memory and experience is stored within its walls. Those thoughts can be turned into emotions. It seems that the conscious mind can only keep a few thoughts in it at one time and that we are largely driven by the unconscious mind.

Since working in the leadership development area, I have had the chance to observe the brain's workings with many people from all walks of life and I am in total awe of it. The way it can retrieve memories from long ago and connect thoughts is incredible. I make brief notes when I am working with clients because I know, when I am working with them again, that those

123

few words will bring all of the necessary information flooding back to me within milliseconds.

As someone who writes, it is even more phenomenal. I see the way in which the brain not only retrieves information and prepares it, but it is like a coffee percolator; I think of a topic I want to write about, and within a couple of days – it's there. My mind has gone to work, compiling relevant data ready for delivery. I am not consciously thinking about it – I am doing other things and just getting on with my day – but my mind is busy beavering away in the background. When the time is right and I *know* that it is, I have to be close to my laptop: the words I need will not wait, and will leave just as quickly as they came, never to be seen in the same way again. I look at the prose and I think it is incredible. There they are – ready for publishing – they are perfect and beautiful. All I have to do is think about the topic and my mind does the rest. I just start writing and it flows. After about 10 minutes, between 500 and 800 words have been

124

written. Very little editing is required. How does this happen? It is just phenomenal. We have a resource within our head that is so powerful, so incredible, and I am sure that we all underutilise it because we are oblivious of our and its potential.

As I started to consciously harness my brain's capacity, it felt like a slow awakening. In my mid-20s, I became dissatisfied with my life. I started on a personal development quest and had no idea what to do or where I would find relevant information. I did not know what I needed or wanted to change – I just knew it was time.

125

I was hungry for knowledge and went to many seminars and workshops, spent much time listening to tapes, read books, and spoke to people I thought could assist me in moving forward. It took two years before I noticed any change at all and it was frustrating. However, I persevered because I did not want to pass on unwanted behaviour patterns to my family.

By the time I was 30 I expected that I would have done enough and I would then be right. After all I, had been doing this thing called 'personal development' for four years now, surely that should be long enough. I was in for a rude shock, because it took much longer than that. It was like peeling an onion – the further down I went, the more layers I uncovered, and the more I needed to do.

126

As luck would have it, years later when I was watching a science program, my ears pricked up and I paid close attention to what was being said. Those being interviewed were talking about cognitive behaviour therapy (CBT), what it is, where it came from, and how it works. I had not heard this term before, and the information was music to my ears. The process described exactly what I had been doing for all of these years – I could now put a name to it and learn much more. The central tenet to CBT is that how we think (cognition), how we feel (emotion), and how we act (behaviour) all interact together.

While Albert Ellis, an American cognitive behavioural therapist developed Rational Emotive Behaviour Therapy in 1955 and is considered by many to be the grandfather of CBT, it was in the 1960s that Aaron T. Beck identified that long-term psycho dynamic approaches based on gaining insight into unconscious emotions and drives had their limitations. He came to the conclusion that his client's perceptions and automatic thoughts (cognitions) were a valuable contribution to the process and could be used in formulating a solution.

127

Over the course of my life, I have found it easy to get stuck in thoughts, and at times the thoughts just keep zooming around in my mind - like a broken record. The process I learned using CBT principles has enabled me to realise that they are just *thoughts* and, while they are annoying, they will not become anything unless I take action. A more pragmatic approach enables me not to get caught up in the thought or to assign it an emotion, and then not to allow it to dominate my thoughts and control my actions, keeping me from getting caught up drama. The thoughts are still there, but I do not step inside of them. It seems that when I focus on a problem, it makes it worse; when I just get on with my work and day, the problems seem to fade away and stop dominating my mind. I know now that if I am having 'one of those days', I can either let my thoughts wreak havoc and things just get worse, or I can stop it right there, change my attitude, and just get on with it. Taking my mind off that mood and not assigning anything to it changes the way I feel and I end up having the best day possible. When my stress levels are low, I manage this easily. However, when my stress levels are high, I have significantly less success.

Scratch the surface of any human being and you will find insecurities; anxieties, and a whole raft of issues that the owner would rather were not there. Many people I have spoken to think that everyone else has it all together and that they are the only ones who have a mind that drives them nuts at times. It is almost like a *secret* that they have never shared with anyone else because they have been too scared to do so in fear of being thought crazy. When I tell them that this seems to be normal for most of us, you should see the look on their face – they are so relieved that finally someone has told them this. It is liberating news.

I AM NOT MY THOUGHTS

129

To me, the positive parenting analogy is what CBT is all about.

Think about a parent we would all love to have had who is functional and has a clear idea about how to raise their children. They are focused, switched on, have done considerable personal development, and continue to evolve. They know that their child has certain abilities at certain ages and that the adult brain is not fully formed until they are 26, hence they do not expect adult behaviour from a baby, child, or adolescent. They guide the child and have realistic expectations. When there is need for discipline, they will tell their child why what they did was wrong regardless of how young or old the child is, how they can fix it, and then monitor the progress. They will often acknowledge things that the kids do well. They will be kid-led to a certain degree and will observe what the child likes and is good at and then provide ample opportunities for them to develop their natural abilities.

As a parent and adult, they know that they will have their good and bad days and they will allow themselves that freedom. It will always be their intention to do the very best they can to empower their children, to hold them accountable for their actions, and to help them to be strong, resilient, emotionally intelligent, happy, decent human beings. As their child progresses from one stage to the next, they will expect them to behave age appropriately and allow them to learn from their mistakes. They will know when to stand back and when to intervene. The long-term plan is for their child to take personal responsibility of their behaviour and actions, and they will never expect themselves or their child to be perfect.

131

While most people would love to have been raised like this, the reality is not enough are. When life doesn't deliver what we want or we didn't have the parents we think we should have, we can end up feeling as though we are hard done by and become negative. This in turn can lead us to becoming cynical, bitter, and twisted (CBT1). We can blame everyone for our life and not put the effort into becoming who we would love to be. The process in CBT enables anyone the opportunity to re-parent themselves and to know that, as an adult, we can no longer blame others for how we turned out or for what we do not like about the world.

I try to remain like the gorgeous little three-year-old, but with the maturity and wisdom of an adult, because it helps me to stay positive and young. Little ones do not know what CBT1 is, or have the foresight to know what life may throw at them as they mature. They just get on with their life – right now. They are busy, live in the moment, and each day is a new beginning. They laugh dozens of times, jump up and down for joy, and are easily entertained.

132

I know that if I am willing to invest in myself and change what I do not like then my life can be rich. I continue to practise this every day and keep up to date with latest findings and weave relevant bits into my life. I choose not to subscribe to CBT1 values or principles because they offer me nothing except to be a miserable person who thinks that I have been hard done by and that others and the world owe me. At all times, when I am aware that CBT1 thoughts have slipped under my radar, I take care of it because that is not how I choose to live my life. There is enough research to show that having a good attitude and being positive does impact favourably on your physical, emotional, and mental health.

Looking back, I am very grateful that I had the foresight in my mid-20s to forge ahead with personal and professional development, fostering this person who is determined to unpack who I am as a human being and always move to the next level. Reviewing this over the years, it was interesting to learn that what I had been practising had been coined CBT by a practitioner in the USA. This technique proved invaluable while recovering from burnout and I am committed to harnessing this power in every area of my life. Without it, I don't know where I would be now. The more I learn about what is possible, the more enthralled I am; the more successes I have, the more confidence it gives me to try other things.

133

10
LIVING LIFE
& LOVING IT

I never expected to burnout and I certainly never expected to be as ill as I was. I am not the type of person who gives up, and the burnout period discussed in this book was confronting, challenging, and bizarre. It was always my goal to reclaim my health. I had much more to do. The book is confronting when I re-read it because I cannot relate to that person I'm writing about anymore. I cannot imagine why or how I allowed myself to become like that in the first place. I cannot believe I did not take notice of the many signs that were right in front of my face. I am staggered by how long it took me to work it out and how long it took me to regain my health. The only reason I have spent the hours it takes to write and update this book is because of **YOU** and anyone else who thinks that they may be burnt out or on the way.

I'm pretty tough and not much daunts me; I have the same amount of fear as anyone else, but I do not allow that to stop me from pursuing my goals and dreams. I expect to achieve my goals and I will do what is necessary to do so. I know my confidence will

135

increase in time when I'm learning something new. I expect to have plenty of energy and I'm not put off by hard work. In this chapter, I identify some of the key strategies used to reclaim my health. You can read the stories from my clients in their chapters, but your story will be your own. The way you reclaim your health will be determined by you and only you. You will have to piece together what is happening, work it out, determine what you will and will not do, and be clear as to what you will and will not accept. Write it down, keep notes, and have your personal weekly meeting but don't give up. You are important, your life is valuable, and when you have reclaimed your life, you can share your knowledge with other people and help them to do the same.

There were many fantastic things that did occur along the way and that I had worked hard for. They were significant in assisting me to remain focused, staying with it, being strategic and goal centred, and maintaining my positive attitude. As time marched on, I noticed that there were things I could do that did make a difference. At that stage, they were not automatic responses and I decided to write them down and formulate a plan. Trying to lighten the situation up, I called it my 'Happy Plan'. The plan was fantastic because the information was just *there* and I did not have to think about it – I could read it and follow it. It put a smile on my face each time I read the name. It had opened another door and I believed that I was moving in the right direction.

I structured each day and had outcomes to achieve linked directly to my long-term objectives. This process was powerful. Whether I completed few things or many it did not matter: I ticked each activity off as I completed it and focused on my goals. My Happy Plan became integral.

137

A holistic way of life has been important to me for years and I have worked hard to be healthy – physically, emotionally, and mentally. On the downward spiral of burnout, something changed. While I continued to eat properly and do what had worked in the past, I was getting sick regularly. It seemed that one virus or cold would go, and within a short time I would get another. It was obvious that good food, exercise, and positive attitude alone was not enough. In order to change this, I saw my holistic practitioner, had regular deep-tissue remedial massages, osteopath treatments, saunas, and spas. I could feel the immediate benefit of the sauna and spa: it helped me relax and have a good sleep. Throughout this time, my body craved carbohydrates and anything else that would give me energy, but I did not succumb. I ensured that I ate properly.

138

Music was played day-in, day-out – sometimes for 10 minutes, other times for hours. Comforting and beautiful, it is surprising that one particular track is still operational because it was played so much. *Blake*, a classical vocal quartet from the United Kingdom is made up of four young men. My favourite track, *Hallelujah* (Blake 2007), gave me a sense of inner peace each time it played. It is clear from the way these young men sing and perform that they put every bit of themselves into the composition and delivery of their music. I will always be grateful to *Blake* for firstly taking the time to develop their genetic gifts and then to share them with the world. They will never know how important they have been to me or be aware of the major impact they have had on my return to health.

I needed to bring fun back into my life. Firstly, because I missed it, but also because I know the benefits of a good laugh – it activates endorphins. Putting myself on a *soft* diet, I was careful of what I viewed on television, read, or listened to. Comedies, kids programs, and feel good movies became my mainstay. This allowed the adrenalin and emotions to settle and made a huge difference to my nervous system. Another move in the right direction.

It never ceases to amaze me what a couple of hours of writing can do to change my mood, and in the burnout period particularly something magical happened when I was writing; the words flowed, my brain focused on something else, and within a few hours I could feel my emotions settling down. My mood lifted

139

and I could complete other things. I felt a sense of great relief and hope for the future. It enabled me to take control of my emotions while doing something I loved – the results were tangible and linked to my long-term objectives.

I had the privilege of being able to attend President Obama's inauguration and to stay in Washington DC for a few days to enjoy the many celebrations that were occurring at this momentous time in history. It is a moment I will never forget. To be standing on the hill in the freezing cold with hundreds of thousands of other people was history in the making. As President Obama said many times throughout his presidency in the White House: 'be the change you want to see.' I then had a break in New York to enjoy that incredible city. It all seemed like a fairy tale. Prior to the trip, my second book, *Sex in the Boardroom*, had been published, and a few months after returning, *The Washington Post* published an article I had written.

ON THE HOMEWARD BOUND
TRIP, THIS IS WHAT I ENTERED
IN MY NOTEBOOK: AWAKENING
TO A MAGNIFICENT SUNRISE,
THE COLOURS WERE RICH AND
BEAUTIFUL AND I FELT AT ONE
WITH MYSELF. AS TEARS ROLLED
DOWN MY CHEEKS, I REFLECTED
ON MY TIME IN THE USA. I FELT AN
INNER PEACE I HAD NOT FELT FOR
A LONG TIME AND KNEW I WAS ON
MY WAY BACK TO HEALTH.

141

Having an article published in *The Washington Post*
had been on my mind for years. This is a big ask and
I had no idea whether it would ever materialise, but it
was worth working towards. When the conversations
and emails were occurring, to say I was surprised
would be an understatement. I was just about jumping
up and down for joy. Changes can occur at the last
minute to an editing schedule for any number of
reasons, and I had taught myself to keep an emotional
lid on it until the goal has been achieved. Given I
work in leadership and the world was in the midst of
the worst global financial crisis since WWII, it was an
opportunity for me to write about it. And it did happen.
The day came, the date arrived. I checked in the email
and there it was - my article had been published in
The Washington Post. Wow. It was wonderful and a
moment that I will never forget. I can still remember
this as though it were yesterday; the article gave
leaders 'five tips on how to survive the global financial
crisis' (The Washington Post 2009). I am delighted
that this goal finally came true, and when I look at the

142

article I still think: *wow that really happened.* Another magical moment and another move in the right direction.

The burnout period saw me spend an inordinate amount of time by myself. In order to compensate for that, I made my home my sanctuary. I love my home anyway, so that was not hard to do. I turned the front room into a studio so that I could work in it and feel part of the community, and where I could enjoy the ever-changing views from the bay window. The view is always beautiful - no matter what time of the day or year, and can transport me to anywhere I want. In the heat of the summer the foliage provides shade from the hot, piercing sun – as the next season arrives, and the trees prepare for their winter solitude, the leaves change colour and drop from the tree. Revealing bare branches there is a starkness about the deciduous tree I do not like and while I prefer the cold weather, I look forward to when spring arrives because within a short period of time tiny buds appear which fill the tree with

143

foliage once again. When the sun is going down, I am treated to a glimpse of the sunset; when it is raining, the heavy drops bounce off the bay windows. When the wind is rustling the leaves, I can hear the noise through the branches. A still day brings the sunshine through the window and onto my lap. And all day long, I have the pleasure of listening to birds sing their song.

I was not willing to accept any labels anyone wanted to pin on my lapel which would then determine my future. Other than reclaiming my health, nothing else was good enough. I could detail many other strategies used, however, the point I am making is that I worked it out as I ventured forward. I focused on being positive and strategic in order to work my way back to where I wanted to be. I wrote in my workbook, mentored myself daily, made sure I ate properly, exercised, and did what I knew worked. I modified my Happy Plan as I learned what else worked. I protected myself from parasites and enacted strong personal boundaries.

145

As human beings, we are not given the right or enough information on how to live our best life. I received more instructions with my new smart television than I did with how to unravel my authentic self. I have also observed that much of the information about burnout misses the point.

If you are reading this book because you need some tips on burnout, always remember that you are the project director of your life and, while a return to health can be achieved, it is hard work and requires that you are honest with yourself. There are many people who will tell you what to do, but you need to take note of whether that is what you *want* to do. If not, keep searching for the right professionals. In the interim, take very good care of your mind and body, and be kind to yourself. Let yourself have a break and be pampered. Perhaps this is new to you and it feels odd, but we need to get used to this.

We need to treat ourselves with love, kindness, and compassion – just as we do everyone else in our life.

APPENDIX

LETTER TO YOU

We have had many conversations since we first
worked together, and I know you enjoy hearing how
I manage when faced with difficult situations. You have
said on a number of occasions that I seem so confident
that it is hard for you to believe that I have to deal with
issues that others face, and as I always reply: 'I am just
like anyone else'. I am normal, have many issues to
face, and because I am always striving to get to the
next level, it is a work in action.

149

It is one thing to want something – it is yet another
to be willing to push through all barriers to achieve it.
I had wanted something for a long time, and because
of developing the business, I had put it on hold. With
some time to spare and a different focus, I decided
to pursue it. In the right place at the right time, I went
ahead. Excited and scared, I enjoyed myself and the
possibility of achieving my goal seemed likely. The
thought of actually attaining it after the event sent
me into an emotional spin and my mind took me on a

merry old ride. The situation rekindled many what ifs and reasons as to why I should not pursue it. Some of my old behaviour patterns kicked in without me even being aware of it, that was until Sunday morning while thinking about your next session. I decided to start jotting down notes because I know these words and ideas do not hang around for long – they seem to depart as quickly as they arrive. As I started writing, I became aware of what I had allowed to happen the day before and my gut was churning with fear and anxiety.

150

I find it remarkable that, regardless as to how often I practise new ways of thinking and behaving, it is easy to fall back into old ways of operating without even realising it. At times, when I am breaking through old stuff, I can feel completely powerless – like a child who has no way out of a situation, who has to do as they are told or suffer the consequences. It is easy to get bogged down in the emotions and become paralysed, thinking that I am not moving forward and fearfully stay where I am even though it is not what I want.

Within one-and-a-half hours of starting to think about your session, the issue had resolved itself – I felt fine and back on track, once again in control of my life. Remnants of the emotions were there, but I could handle them and not feel overwhelmed.

When I think like this and get into action, I feel empowered and can take a big deep breath knowing that I do not have to be subjugated by old patterns and other people's agendas. It is my life and I will continue to strive for and achieve my professional and personal goals.

151

I know that each time I look in the mirror, the person looking directly back at me is the only one who can change what they do not like about their life.

We have discussed your natural abilities often and it is early days for you. I know that you don't realise how incredible your genetic gifts are because you have had them for so long that they just seem *normal* to you. I remember when I became aware that I had a natural ability in writing. It took me a long time before I identified it and it was only because of feedback from other people that I did become aware. However, it took many years to develop my skills in this area. When I first started writing articles, it took me days to write a fairly basic, publishable article and my stress levels were high. Now, it takes me much less time and they are of a higher quality. The exciting thing about discovering one genetic gift is that there comes with it a certain confidence and other natural abilities seem to emerge.

You mentioned that you thought you had to go to work and hate what you do just to earn an income - the fact that you could do what you love had never entered your mind. This attitude and belief seems to be dominant in society (at all levels) and if you do happen to love what you do, then it is said that it isn't work. This is one of the reasons I burnt out so badly; when you love what you do, when passion and enthusiasm are running through your veins, you are able to work long hours and not think of it as work. But it *is* work, and the body, emotions, and mind need time to rest and recover. Think about a baby - they play all day and are exhausted by the end of it. They need regular rests and a good sleep otherwise they can become tired and cranky and anyone who has been around a baby like this, knows it is not much fun. Their play is their work, and as adults, whatever we do takes physical, emotional, and mental energy and is therefore work, whether we love or hate it, whether we see it as important or not.

I know that you are working hard and are taking action, and it will take time before you see the results – how long depends on how long you have been behaving in a certain way and how hard you are willing to work.

153

I know that you are frustrated at the moment because change is not happening as quickly as you would like, but unfortunately that is not the way humans work. It takes time to become aware of what we want or need to change, and then much more time (and work) than most of us would like before results are seen. For this reason, it is essential to identify and notice even the smallest change because that is developing those new connections in your brain, and ongoing work adds to it and the branches thicken – the other habits that you do not like as much and the connections they have created are always there but they seem to take a bit of a back seat – until they are stirred up again for whatever reason, of course. When we keep reading, acquiring knowledge that is pertinent to us and keep practising, it keeps building those 'good' connections in the brain and helps us to develop new habits. It is tempting to continue to do what we do every day because it is safe and comfortable (even if we hate the results we have), however, if it is not bringing the results we want, then we need to do things differently.

If, when we are feeling overwhelmed emotionally, we go and do something else, the brain seems to go to work to solve 'the problem' as it did in the situation I speak of in this letter and I have found it also helps me to become centred again. It is the old stuff hitting the new stuff and causing problems. When we keep thinking about the problem, we grow more of the connections that we do not want in our brain. The hardest part is to create the new connections in the first place. I have found that this can take a long time. It is as though that first connection starts the process and when similar new information is brought in, old and new are joined and that is where knowledge about a particular topic occurs and where the (new) learnings come from – commonly called insights.

In essence, it is exactly like a baby learning to walk – they fall over countless times before they master it, and when you observe a baby trying to master the art of eating, you will notice they make a mess for a long time. Then, when you look at them months later, they are proud of themselves because they can do it. But they do not stay with that for long – they master it and move onto bigger and better challenges and then practise that over and over again until they have mastered yet another thing. They are building new connections and branches in their brain, always moving forward, trying new things, and challenges. Babies are not deterred by obstacles because no one has told them they should be, they just want to explore

155

and learn, that is unless those who care for them wrap them up in cotton wool or fill them with fear and anxiety and expect them to behave like mini-adults and criticise them for being just who they are.

Keep moving forward. Keep reviewing and refining what you do and acknowledge yourself for having the courage to be aware that you need to change if you want to continue to pursue your goals and dreams. Acknowledge yourself for the courage and tenacity it takes to stay with the process until you have achieved your desired outcomes.

I wish you well.
Kind regards,

Merydith Willoughby

Executive advisor

www.linkedin.com/in/merydithwilloughby

info@merydithwilloughby.com

New York City 718 790 9729

Australia 61 435086641

BIBLIOGRAPHY

Ammon-Wexler, J 2010, viewed 26 April 2010,
<http://www.canadaone.com/bio/jammon_wexler.html>.

Beck, AT, Hollon, S, Leahy B 2010, 'In discussion at the Association for Behavioural and Cognitive Therapies Annual Conference', USA.

Blake 2007, *Hallelujah*, CD, ASIN:B000TZGQHM.

Darling, D 2003, *The Complete Book of Spaceflight: From Apollo 1 to Zero Gravity"*, John Wiley & Sons, Inc, USA.

Ellis, A 1999, *How to Make Yourself Happy and Remarkably Less Disturbable*. New York: Impact Publishers.

Willoughby, M 2009, 'Five Leadership How-Tos for Recession Survival', *The Washington Post,* June 6th, 2009. <http://views. washingtonpost.com/leadership/leadership_playlist/2009/06/ surviving-the-recession-5-tips-from-merydith-willoughby.html>.

159